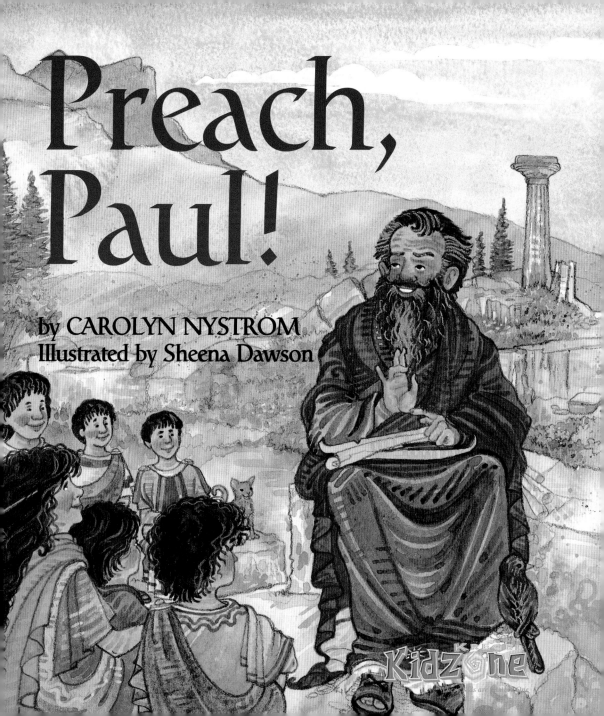

Preach, Paul!

by CAROLYN NYSTROM
Illustrated by Sheena Dawson

Text © 2004 Carolyn Nystrom
Illustrations © 2004 Lion Hudson plc/
Tim Dowley & Peter Wyart trading as Three's Company

Published in the USA by Kregel Publications 2004
Distributed by Kregel Publications,
Grand Rapids, Michigan 49501

Learn more about Paul in the book of Acts, 8:1–3;
9:1–31; 11:25–30; 13:1–28:3.

ISBN 0-8254-3333-9

Worldwide co-edition produced by Lion Hudson plc,
Mayfield House, 256 Banbury Road,
Oxford OX2 7DH,
Tel: +44 (0) 1865 302750
Fax: +44 (0) 1865 302757
e-mail: coed@lionhudson.com
www.lionhudson.com

Printed in China

04 05 06 07 08 / 5 4 3 2 1

When I was a small boy
I liked to run down the road at top speed
and spin a top with a stick and feed my pet sheep
and wrestle my friends.

But I liked one thing more than anything else.
I liked to study.
I went to a special school for Jewish boys.
We read the Bible over and over.
We debated God's laws.
I had the best teacher in the world: Gamaliel.
And I was his best student.

I grew up.
I knew all of God's laws.
I could explain them better than anyone I know.
I hated people who did not do what God said.
I hated people who disagreed with me.
I wanted them dead.

Once I saw a young man kneeling in the street.
"This man talks against God's law," people shouted.
"This man says our temple will fall down,"
they shouted. "He thinks Jesus is God!"
The crowd roared and picked up rocks.

Men threw off their coats
and rolled up their sleeves.
They threw rocks hard and straight—
straight at Stephen.
I took care of their coats.

4

"Lord Jesus, forgive them,"
I heard Stephen whisper.
Then he died.

5

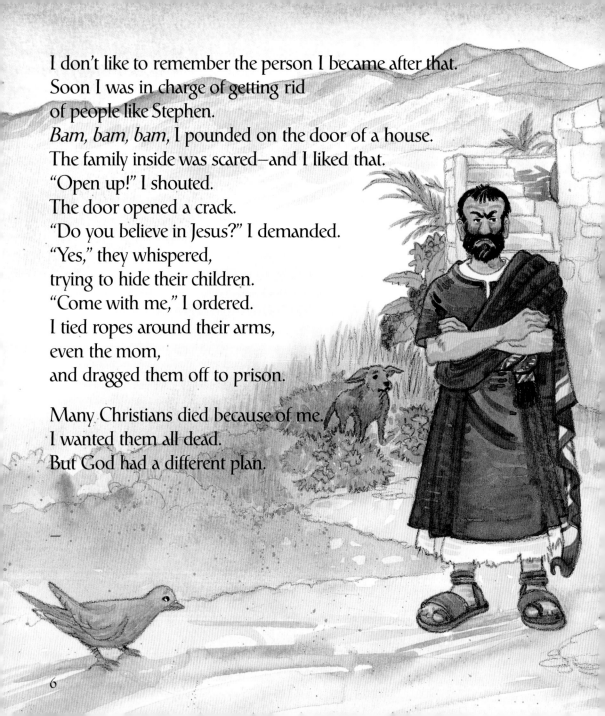

I don't like to remember the person I became after that.
Soon I was in charge of getting rid
of people like Stephen.
Bam, bam, bam, I pounded on the door of a house.
The family inside was scared—and I liked that.
"Open up!" I shouted.
The door opened a crack.
"Do you believe in Jesus?" I demanded.
"Yes," they whispered,
trying to hide their children.
"Come with me," I ordered.
I tied ropes around their arms,
even the mom,
and dragged them off to prison.

Many Christians died because of me.
I wanted them all dead.
But God had a different plan.

Trot, tramp, trot, tramp. I was on my way
to Damascus with letters in my pocket.
Those letters said I could throw all the Jesus-lovers
into prison. "It will be a fun trip," I growled.
What happened next changed me forever.
Suddenly a light flashed from heaven–the brightest light
I had ever seen. I clapped my hands over my eyes
and fell to the ground.
Then a voice boomed, "Saul, Saul, why are you hurting me?"
"Wh-wh-who?" I stammered. (But I knew.)
"Who are you, Lord?" I asked as politely as I could.
"I am Jesus, and you are hurting me,"
came the answer as strong as thunder.
Hurting Jesus? I wondered.
But Jesus is dead–or is he?
"Get up," the voice said. "Go into the city."
"You will be told what to do."
I took my hands away from my face
and found that I was blind.
Friends led me into the city.

For three days I sat and thought and prayed.
I did not eat or drink.
Have I been wrong? I wondered.
I only wanted to make people obey God.
I thought Jesus only pretended to be God.
I thought he was dead.
I thought his people were stupid.

"Lord God," I prayed. "I'm sorry.
Please forgive me."

I heard a knock at the door.
Then I felt a hand on my shoulder.
"Brother Saul," a kind voice said,
"Jesus sent me to you."
"I believe," I said.

Suddenly I could see again.
God's Holy Spirit filled me like a rushing wind.
I asked to be baptized—as a believer in Jesus.

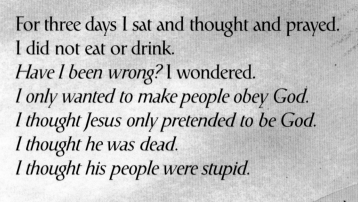

11

"Jesus is the Son of God," I preached.
I stood on street corners, sat in homes,
taught in synagogues.
Everywhere I went
I preached the same message.
"Jesus is God's Son.
He came to earth and taught us how to live.
He died on a cross for our sin.
But Jesus came back to life!
Jesus is alive in heaven."

Jewish leaders were worried.
I knew they were watching me.
Would they try to kill me?

"You've got to leave,"
my new friends whispered.
One night they dumped me
into a deep basket
and lowered me outside the city wall.

I spent the next three years in the desert.
I prayed and thought and studied.
And I got to know Jesus.

Much later I was with my friends
in the church at Antioch.
While we were praying, God said,
"I have a special job for two of you.
You must send Saul and Barnabas
on a long trip. I want them to tell people
who are not Jews about Jesus."
People of the church put their hands on us
and prayed.

My name changed to Paul after that.
I went on three long trips—as God's missionary.
I traveled as far as horses and ships
and my own feet would carry me.
Many friends helped: Barnabas, Mark, Luke,
Silas, Priscilla, Aquila, and many others.
Everywhere I went, I preached about Jesus.
God's Spirit helped people to believe.
Churches began in almost every town.
I knew that God had been getting me ready
to do this work—ever since I was a boy.

15

I loved telling people about Jesus and seeing them believe,
but it wasn't always easy. Our stay in Philippi began well.
We met by the river to pray. Lydia joined us there.
She worked by selling purple cloth in the town.
Lydia worshipped the true God,
but she hadn't heard about Jesus.
"Lydia," I said, "Jesus loves you."
God helped her believe.
I baptized Lydia as a new Christian—
and everyone in her family.
Lydia was so happy about the good news of Jesus
that she invited us to stay in her house
while I told other people about him.

One day I saw a little slave girl in the streets.
Her master used her to make money.
"Put your coins here," he would yell.
"This girl will tell your fortune."
Sometimes what the girl said really did happen.
I could see that the little girl was sad and hurt.
I saw that a bad spirit lived inside her.

Some days the girl chased after us.
She screamed and cried.
I knew she needed help.
Finally I turned around and shouted to the bad spirit,
"In the name of Jesus Christ," I said,
"Come out of her!"

At that moment the girl stopped screaming.
She sat down next to me and smiled.
God had taken away the bad spirit—
but she couldn't tell fortunes any more.

"You wrecked my business,"
yelled the girl's owner.
Men grabbed me and Silas.
"These men are causing trouble,"
they shouted. Someone ripped
off my coat. Someone else grabbed
a whip. I felt hard metal dig
across my back—again and again.
A huge man flung me into jail.
I heard Silas thud in behind me.
Then I heard a door clang shut.
We sat against a cold dark wall
and groaned. But God was
with us. That night we prayed
and sang songs to him.
I knew the other prisoners
were listening.

Suddenly an earthquake shook the whole prison.
All the doors flew open. Our chains fell off.
We could have all walked out—but we didn't.
I stood in the doorway.
The jailer jumped to his feet.
He stared at the open door, and grabbed his sword.
"Stop!" I shouted. "Don't hurt yourself.
We are all here!"

He fell down at my feet.
"What can I do to be saved?" he begged.
"Believe in the Lord Jesus, and you will be saved,"
I answered. "And so will everyone
who lives in your house."

That night the jailer took us to his home.
He washed our sores and gave us supper.
I told him and his family about Jesus.
Everyone believed! I baptized them all.
There was so much joy in heaven that the angels
had a party—and so did we!

After many years of travel and telling people about Jesus,
God's Spirit told me to go back to Jerusalem.
I knew that I might die there.
Many people there were angry
about all the new Christian churches.
They thought preaching about Jesus
was a big mistake.
They were like I was—at first.

"Please don't go," said my friends at Ephesus.
(I had lived there for three years
and worked at making tents.)
"I must finish the job God has given me," I told them.
"But I think you will never see me again.
Take care of the people in your church—
the same way a shepherd takes care of sheep.
Your church is like the body of Jesus."

We knelt on the shore and prayed.
Then I hugged and kissed each one—
and got on the ship.

It happened almost as soon as I got to Jerusalem.
"This man preaches about Jesus all over the world,"
people shouted. "Get him away from our temple! Kill him!"
Roman soldiers carried me over their heads
to save me from the mob.
"Let me speak to the people," I begged.
With soldiers all around me, I told my story
and I preached about Jesus.

I spent more than two years in jail.
I had four trials.
At each trial, I talked about Jesus.
I hoped that those who heard
would become Christians.
"I'll think about it later," said Governor Felix.
Finally, King Agrippa and his wife came to visit.
They wanted to know why I was in jail.
All the leaders of the town came with them to hear me.
Of course, I talked about Jesus.
"Do you think you can convince me to be a Christian?"
grumbled the king.
"I wish everyone here believed as much as I do,"
I answered.
I knew that if I got out of jail I would be killed.
"Send me to Rome," I said.

27

Rome was more than a thousand miles away.
As I got on a ship with other prisoners,
I felt the cold wind of early winter
and knew it could be a long and dangerous trip.

Soon a vicious storm tore at our sails.
Sailors tightened ropes under the boat.
Wind tore the sails to shreds.
Sailors threw out a sea anchor.
Waves tossed us up and down.
Sailors threw the cargo overboard.
We sank deeper into the water.
No one had eaten for days.

One night, as I pitched back and forth on my cot,
an angel stood beside me.
"Don't be afraid," he said. "God wants you in Rome.
No one will die who sails with you."

"Men," I said the next day,
 "my God gave me good news.
Don't be afraid; no one will die.
But," I added a little sadly,
"the ship will go down."

29

The storm raged for two weeks.
One night at midnight, the sailors discovered land ahead.
They dropped four anchors and prayed for morning.
I heard the ship creaking through the night
and knew it wouldn't hold together much longer.
Just before dawn, I called the frightened men together.
"Eat," I said. "No one will lose a single hair today."
Then I thanked God for our food.
A piece of the deck crashed into the water.

The sun hovered just above the ocean
and shined on the best possible sight.
Land! An island!

With the ship's last energy,
the captain aimed straight for the shore,
scattering pieces of ship along the way.
Crash! We slapped onto the beach.
Crunch! The boat splintered in half.

"Shouldn't we kill the prisoners?" shouted a soldier.
My guard glanced at me. "No," he shouted.
"Grab a board and swim!"
Soon we were warming ourselves by a fire–every one of us.
We stayed the winter on the island of Malta.
In the spring, we took another ship headed north.

I am telling my story from Rome.
I cannot leave my house, because I am a prisoner.
But many people come to visit—and to hear about Jesus.
I write letters to my friends in churches
all over the world.
Even though I am a prisoner, I can still work for God.
And I am happy.
Here is a note from one of my letters:
I live by faith in the Son of God,
who loved me and gave himself for me.
—Galatians 2:20b